SLA GUIDELINES

Establishing a
Secondary School
Library Policy

Elspeth Scott

Third edition
Published by the School Library Association
Liden Library, Barrington Close
Liden, Swindon SN3 6HF
© School Library Association 1996
Printed by Willprint, Oxford

Introduction

The demands of the present-day curriculum require pupils to have access to a wide range of materials. The library is the ideal place for these information resources and for acquiring the study skills necessary for success in school, in further education and in adult life. The development of educational technology has meant that libraries are now expected to stock a range of resources embracing slides, tapes, filmstrips, videos, computer software, CD-ROM, and on-line information services such as Campus World; and to provide access to the Internet. Thus a school library is indeed a multimedia centre, co-ordinating resources throughout the school, providing an apt environment for learning, and ensuring that pupils (and staff) acquire the skills to locate and use information; and providing, too, fiction and recreational material.

Such a library does not simply happen. It requires commitment and perseverance from the librarian and the school management, and willing co-operation from both pupils and teachers. The base from which all developments will spring is a good library policy — that is to say, a clear written statement which sets out:

(a) the role of the library/resource centre within the school

(b) the aims of the service and the means of implementation

(c) the roles and responsibilities of the staff.

Such a policy will ensure that the place of the library in the school's educational philosophy is clearly understood, and that:

> 'The library is not aside from, or a buttress to the curriculum, but its skills are the very foundation of the curriculum.' [1]

---

[1] *School Libraries: the Foundations of the Curriculum*. Report of the Library and Information Services Council's Working Party on School Library Services (LISC Report). Office of Arts and Libraries, HMSO, 1984.

The Case for a School Library Policy

It is easy to assume that everyone in the school knows and understands the aims and objectives of the library. Unfortunately this is frequently not the case. Most specialists will see the library in relation to their own subject (for example, the English department may see it primarily as a provider of recreational reading, while the maths department may not appreciate its relevance at all); but with the recent emphasis on resource-based learning and the investigative approaches of GCSE and Standard Grade, a narrow view is not enough. The central educational role of the library must be clearly understood by all to ensure a full and effective use of resources.

The need for a coherent library policy is increased by the recent introduction of formal development planning into schools, and the consequent need for departments, including the library, to produce individual development plans.[2] An effective library development plan will arise naturally from the library policy, which in turn will be affected by the priorities established. The two are thus interdependent and mutually supportive.

The development of a policy for the school library involves taking a close look at what the users and potential users of the service require. This can be a salutary experience for the librarian, who should not make assumptions about requirements. The teaching staff's perceptions of what a library is and can do may not match up with those of the librarian. What are the needs of the users? To what extent are they being met by existing resources and services? Both sides will learn much from this exercise — not least that they are not in opposition but are partners in a team, aiming to implement the policies of the school.

It is essential that this policy should be written. An 'unwritten' policy, like an unwritten constitution, is capable of many interpretations according to what each person thinks it is. The very act of writing the policy will clarify thoughts, and having an actual document to circulate has several advantages:

> (a) copies can be given to every member of staff and any other relevant bodies (the Inspectorate, the governors or the School Board, for example). New members of staff will automatically receive a copy.

> (b) everyone will have the same information and, if it is properly expressed, the same understanding of the library's role.

> (c) any questions will be easily answered and misunderstandings cleared up.

> (d) a formal written policy to which reference can be made will simplify decision-making.

---

[2] See *Development Planning for the School Library Resource Centre*. SLA Guideline. School Library Association, 1993.

These are the practical advantages. There are also three philosophical advantages in producing a school library policy document:

1. It will clarify the role of the library within the school, and within the community

The differing perceptions which departments may have of the library's role have already been mentioned, but the question is more fundamental. The library is an integral part of the school and the policy should make this clear. It is an essential part not only of resources but also of the educational process; not simply a curriculum support but also an initiator and developer. A policy which ensures that all staff are aware of the potential role of the library should lead to closer integration of the library into the educational methods of the school. The library is also part of a wider network and will have links with other libraries and institutions, and increasingly with feeder primaries. These links too will be improved by a clear policy.

2. It will provide a means of evaluating the service and a reasoned basis for development

The policy document provides a firm statement of what the library should be doing, against which its actual performance can be measured. It will provide a basis for establishing the performance indicators and quality measurements which schools are now being asked to introduce, and indeed such performance indicators may be included in the policy statement. The document will be, in many ways, a statement of the ideal, so that at each evaluation an improvement should be looked for, a closer match with the users' needs. These evaluations can themselves act as another weapon in the battle for adequate resources and staffing. From analysis and evaluation of the present situation it will be possible to make a phased plan for the future development of the service, following a carefully constructed order of priority.

3. It will strengthen claims for resources and staffing

The LISC Report and the SLA and LA Guidelines (see Recommended Reading) have all made recommendations for staffing and resource levels, fully implemented by very few schools even in the most advanced authorities. A policy will show by how much the school is falling short of what needs to be provided. A library with a higher profile, and a better understanding by the staff of its value, will have a better chance of adequate funding. The librarian will be able to base budget estimates on the actual, expressed needs of the users, and the requirements of the policy will help to assess the necessary levels of staffing. Job descriptions may be tied in with the policy, thus clarifying the roles of the librarian and the support staff.

How to Draw Up a Policy Statement

It is not possible to draw up and issue a standard library policy, since a policy document is particular to the situation in a given school. Factors which have to be taken into account are:

1. The educational philosophy of the school — what are its aims and how does it try to achieve them? These, in turn, are likely to be affected by national educational trends, by the policies of the LEA, or by local circumstances (being in an area of social or economic deprivation, for example).

2. The existence, or otherwise, of support services for the library, whether through education departments or through the public library.

3. Any formal links with primary or tertiary education.

4. The internal arrangements of the school. Some constraints may be physical — split sites, cramped or overcrowded premises, libraries used as classrooms.

   — Are these long-term or temporary situations?

   — Will falling rolls turn split sites into single sites, or free other space for the library?

Other constraints are managerial — organisation of the curriculum, timetabling of 'study' periods for older pupils, the basis on which funding is allocated.

   — Is the library funded as a whole-school resource or as an extra?

   — Are there existing policies on resources or information skills?

   — Are there existing links between the library and teaching?

The importance of consultation

For the librarian to attempt to develop the school library policy in isolation is counter-productive. The first step is to involve colleagues on the teaching staff. A Library Committee, if one already exists, is an obvious starting point. If not, approach the head or the school's senior management team; ask if time may be made available at a staff meeting to put the case for a school library policy. Once the staff have been won over to the idea — and majority support is essential — there must be consultation with governors on the one hand and pupils on the other. Perhaps a working party needs to be appointed — but make sure it does *work*.

Surveying the scene

Having decided who is to draw up the document, the next step is to look at the current situation, bearing in mind the factors already mentioned. A library policy should be consistent with any existing school policies, and the school's declared aims may form a useful basis for establishing aims and objectives for its library. Look at the position of the library within the school. What is the chain of command? What are the present links with the teaching staff? How does the library support the school in delivering the curriculum? Is the library regarded as an important educational resource or is it peripheral?

The recent rapid and substantial increase in affordable information technology, including databases, and especially the almost universal introduction of CD-ROM in schools, has had a major impact on school library resource centres. These tools, as whole-school resources, are most usually located in the library and this, coupled with the fact that librarians have been quicker to realise and begin to exploit their potential, has resulted in the librarian effectively becoming the school expert on information technology for information retrieval and management. Even if the role of the library/ librarian is acknowledged in the school IT policy, it is important for the library policy to take account of these developments and to make explicit the rationale behind the library's/librarian's role. This is even more important if there is no IT policy.

Identifying the needs of the users

Determine first who the users actually are. Pupils and staff? Subjects and departments? Consider, too, any outside bodies who may use the service — feeder primary schools or the local community.

Identify the needs of both actual and potential users. It is no use making assumptions about what is wanted. While it may be fairly straightforward to induce present users, already well disposed towards the library, to discuss their needs, it will be more difficult to establish what will most help those not currently using the library. Some may not appreciate that the service can be of any relevance to them if it is currently falling short of their needs.

How are needs to be established?

Consultation and discussion with individuals are time consuming and could lead to inconsistencies in eliciting and recording information. The advantage is that many people are more amenable to a friendly, personal approach — if this can be fitted into a crowded timetable. Less time consuming for the researcher, though not for the respondent, is the use of a carefully constructed questionnaire, which ensures a consistent approach to the collection of information. There is, however, no way of ensuring that everyone will take the time or trouble to complete a questionnaire thoughtfully so that the results are valid.

It may be possible to use school-based in-service time for this part of the process, using whatever combination of methods seems the most appropriate. Look at needs under the following headings:

Accommodation

— Facilities for: individual study
                          group study/class use
                          use of non-book materials

— Adequate shelving/storage for books/non-book material

Are resources centralised or scattered throughout the school, and, in the given school, which should they be?

Resources

— Is there enough stock of reasonable quality?

— Is it up to date, attractive, relevant, suitable in age/ability range?

— Who is responsible for selecting resources?

— Who else should be involved?

— Are special sections required (local collections, careers library, staff library) which may need special consideration? If they do not exist at present, should they?

Access

— Who has access to the library?

— What control should there be?

— Are there any restrictions on numbers — of pupils or groups?

— How much access is there out of school hours?

— What about holidays?

Services

— Reference/enquiry service

— Curriculum involvement (such as advisory role when new courses are developed)

— Provision of resources lists to meet individual or departmental needs

— Co-ordinating resources within the school

— Instruction in library/information skills as required

— Guidance for pupils in investigation work

— Current awareness service for staff/pupils

— Provision of bibliographic information/advice on suitability of material

— Obtaining material not available within school.

These needs will be affected by the school's attitude to the role of resources. If there is a strong emphasis on resource-based learning and self-supported study, for example, there are major implications for the library.

Once needs have been identified, they can be matched against current provision to find where the service falls short. Priorities can be established and a development plan drawn up. For successful implementation of the policy, targets must be realistic, and may have to be phased in gradually; an over-ambitious or over-hasty attempt to implement a policy may well lead to disappointment and disillusionment.

The policy will need to be regularly reviewed and may from time to time require revision in the light of educational trends and developments in teaching approaches. TVEI, the National Curriculum, and the rapid growth of educational technology all have implications for the needs of library users.

Writing the Policy Document

The final step in establishing the aims of the library is to put together the identified needs of the users with the aims of the school. At this stage, it would be helpful to look again at the general guidelines which have been drawn up by bodies such as the SLA, LISC, LISC (Scotland), the LA, and the Scottish LA (see Recommended Reading).

It is likely that the following points will have to be covered in the policy document:

(a) the library as a source of all forms of learning materials for staff and pupils, for use by individuals, small groups and whole classes, in response to the needs of the curriculum, and cultural and recreational interests;

(b) the library as a source of information about learning and teaching materials throughout the school (through a central catalogue);

(c) the library's role in acquiring and disseminating information to all staff on materials for professional needs;

(d) the library's role in developing information skills throughout the school and in enabling resources to be fully exploited;

(e) the library's role in consulting with and supporting teaching staff on the selection of materials appropriate to their learning objectives;

(f) the library's role in curriculum development within the school and with appropriate outside bodies;

(g) the library as a means of access for pupils and staff to outside agencies and sources of information;

(h) the library's role in the provision and organisation of equipment for use with audio-visual and non-book materials, and of reprographic facilities within the school;

(i) the library's role in encouraging recreational reading.

Using the same structure as existing school policy documents will make for consistency, clarity and ready acceptance of new proposals. Once it has been drawn up, copies of the policy statement should be widely distributed; a policy is useful only if it is known about, understood and acted upon.

It is even more true today than it was twenty years ago that the library is 'at the heart of the school's resources for learning.' [3] The existence and implementation of a good library policy will ensure continuation of this principle and will immensely benefit the school.

---

[3] *A Language for Life*. Report of the Committee of Enquiry under the Chairmanship of Sir Alan Bullock (Bullock Report). Department of Education and Science, HMSO, 1975.

Recommended Reading

DE SILVA, RUFUS *School Library Resource Centre Policy: Policy Guidelines for Development.*
Grampian Regional Council, 1991. 1 873019 10 6

DE SILVA, RUFUS and TURRIFF, ALISON *Developing the Secondary School Resource Centre.*
Kogan Page, 1993. 0 7494 0819 7

DUNNE, JOHN *Establishing a Primary School Library Policy.* SLA Guideline. School Library
Association, 1994. 0 900641 69 X

KING, ELIZABETH *The School Library: Responding to Change.* Northcote House, 1989.
0 7463 0517 6

KINNELL, MARGARET (Editor) *Learning Resources in Schools: Library Association Guidelines
for School Libraries.* Library Association, 1992. 1 85604 032 1

KINNELL, MARGARET (Editor) *Managing Library Resources in Schools.* Library Association,
1994. 1 85604 096 8

LISC *School Libraries: the Foundations of the Curriculum.* Office of Arts and Libraries, 1984. 0 11
630713 7

LISC (SCOTLAND) *Library Services and Resources for Schools Education in Scotland.* LISC
(Scotland), 1985. 0 948705 00 0

PAIN, HELEN and LESQUEREUX, JOHN *Developing a policy for a school library.* 2nd edn.
School Libraries Group of the Library Association, 1987. 0 948933 00 3

ROBERTSON, STEWART *Development Planning for the School Library Resource Centre.* SLA
Guideline. School Library Association, 1993. 0 900641 67 3

SCHOOL LIBRARY ASSOCIATION *School Libraries: Steps in the Right Direction.* 1989.
0 900641 51 7

SCOTTISH CENTRE FOR EDUCATION AND TRAINING 'Writing Policy Statements'. Unit 5 in
Effective Management: a Guide for Middle Managers in Schools. Strathclyde Region/SCET/
Department of Employment Training Agency, 1989. 0 86011 153 9 (Available from SCET.)

SCOTTISH EDUCATION DEPARTMENT 'Aims, Objectives and Policies'. Unit 2 in *Principles of
Management* (part of a *Management Training for Headteachers* pack). HMSO, 1990. 0 7480
0345 2

SCOTTISH LIBRARY ASSOCIATION *The School Library Resource Service and the Curriculum.*
1985. 0 900649 57 7

WRIGHT, VIVIAN 'Formulating library policy' in *School Libraries in Action*, edited by Margaret
Kinnell. Taylor Graham, 1994. 0 947568 65 4

Notes